SOMETIMES I LAUGH LIKE

Rebecca Peyton and Martin M. Bartelt

SOMETIMES I LAUGH
LIKE MY SISTER

OBERON BOOKS
LONDON

WWW.OBERONBOOKS.COM

First published in 2012 by Oberon Books Ltd
521 Caledonian Road, London N7 9RH
Tel: +44 (0) 20 7607 3637 / Fax: +44 (0) 20 7607 3629
e-mail: info@oberonbooks.com
www.oberonbooks.com

A catalogue record for this book is available from the British
Library.

ISBN: 978-1-8494-3186-6

Front cover image by Adam Levy
Back cover image by Michele Engeler

Printed and bound by CPI Group (UK) Ltd, Croydon, CR0 4YY.

For Mum and Charles
and Kate and Dad,
for the inspiration, the love, the rigour
Rebecca Peyton

To the people I met on my way and who gave
me the inspiration to become who I am today
Martin M. Bartelt

CONTENTS

INTRODUCTION

I don't remember when exactly, but it was within days of Kate's death that I knew I wanted to make some kind of show out of my experiences. The first idea was entitled *101 Uses For A Murdered Sister* and comprised many of the extraordinary and mundane things I'd had the chance to do because of her death and the nature of it – from meeting Ban Ki-moon, through flying first class with British Airways, to sobbing on the tube in the middle of the day while I felt those around me burying themselves deeper in their newspapers. But however much I wanted to make something, I knew I was adrift.

Then, two and a half years into my post-Kate world, I met Martin. He was teaching on a course which I attended at the Actors Centre. At the end of the course he said he'd like to work with me. I said I was only interested in making a show about Kate. He said, 'Great.' And so we started making something.

With Martin based in Switzerland and me in London the work has involved a great deal of travelling. The first time I went out to stay with him, in a tiny village in the Italian part of Switzerland, driving through the darkened, winding mountain roads I wondered what on earth I was doing. I had no idea where in Switzerland I was, where I was going, let alone any metaphorical idea of where I was going. The terrible, rudderless maelstrom of a life without my best friend – my future – could this insubstantial craft really take the weight of some kind of writing process and performance?

For Martin, it was not until we were in the theatre he was then running in Switzerland that he felt sure we could make a show. I was on stage, he was being the demanding director in the stalls, and we worked with some of my story, Martin asking more and more of me as a performer. It was at this point that it became clear to him that I could separate the part of me which was grieving for Kate from the performer, and writer, to work with the material as though it were just that: a story.

People ask how I could bear to be submerged in this material. My answer is that I have been neck-deep in my sister's murder and its repercussions, unable to think about anything else, for years. Making *Sometimes I Laugh Like My Sister* was to be productive with the endless churning, the numberless tiny little adjustments which comprise some of the hard work of grief. Martin was interested in what are, frankly, the tedious minutiae of the grief-stricken, in the repetition, in what might resonate as universal and what was specific to me.

Through all the listening and talking we soon discovered that we share a vision of what theatre can do with people's real stories. I have adopted much of Martin's technique, including the idea that if either of us needs to stop working at any moment, then we do. I don't want to make us sound lazy, but it was the only way we could work with such personal material, be creatively honest and at the same time stay the best of friends.

I found myself very drained and distracted by the years of preparations for Kate's inquest, exacerbated the BBC's attempts to close down the parameters which the Coroner had set for his enquiry. And so when the inquest finally ended in December 2008 it was a relief to get to work in earnest. Martin had met my family, which was very important to him, and some of Kate's friends in the run up to this point as preparation for the project.

We put down eight and a half hours of material on video, which we edited and finally, moving our schedule around to allow for Martin to have his heart valve replaced in July, performed in Switzerland in December 2009. We have since given several performances in Switzerland, made the version which we performed in Edinburgh in 2010 and took on a thirty-one date tour in 2011, and created the version you read here for the London premiere at the Finborough Theatre in January 2012.

There are many questions which we are asked time and again. One of them is whether I stick to a script, to a structure, or whether I'm just talking. Delighted as we are that sometimes people feel I am just chatting to them, it can muddy the waters for audiences about what they are seeing. We know very clearly they are seeing a performance of a play, I could not have done it otherwise. And we hope we have written a play which others might perform.

Yet this wondering what on earth I am doing has never really left me, it waxes and wanes, but for me it is the leitmotif of this work. Martin was always far clearer that we could make a show and when I have entirely lost faith, he has remained clear that we can make something, and make something which needed to be made.

Of course, Martin has been vindicated. We have been overwhelmed by the desire of people to stay and talk to us after the show, we have heard so many incredible stories from audience members, as Martin says, everyone has a story to tell.

I was greeting audience members post-show one day in Edinburgh. A woman came up to me, 'Thank you so much,' she said, shaking me by the hand, 'You have helped me grieve for my father.' It was pretty early on in the run, before I had come to understand the power of what we had made, 'Thank you,' I said, 'that's more than we ever hoped for.' 'Yes,' she said, 'he died thirty years ago' I couldn't imagine what our modest, honest show had done that this woman had not found for thirty years.

This has encouraged us to start work on new projects, involving the extraordinary stories which we all hold, because people are amazing.

Rebecca Peyton,
December 2011

Sometimes I Laugh Like My Sister was first performed on 10th December 2009 at Teatro Paravento, Locarno, Switzerland. We then toured it to many other Swiss venues.

A shorter version of the show ran between 4th-30th August 2010 at The Pleasance, Edinburgh Festival Fringe, and was then toured nationally and to France in 2011.

Sometimes I Laugh Like My Sister received its London premiere on 8th January 2012 at The Finborough Theatre, London. The version herein has been created for the London run.

These performances of *Sometimes I Laugh Like My Sister* were produced by Vital Digression and Obviam Est.

Although we always knew who would be performing the first outings of *Sometimes I Laugh Like My Sister* we also always hoped others might be interested in working with it. We are very curious how the show might develop with others working on it, and, of course, there is nothing stopping a man performing the play.

As for the set and lighting, it needs to be as if the actor just comes in and starts to chat. Therefore, it's important that neither the set nor the lighting is elaborate.

Written by Rebecca Peyton and Martin M. Bartelt
Directed by Martin M. Bartelt
Performed by Rebecca Peyton
Lighting design Martin M. Bartelt
Set design Martin M. Bartelt and Rebecca Peyton

Rebecca Peyton

Rebecca Peyton is a writer and performer. *Sometimes I Laugh Like My Sister* is her playwriting debut. As an actor, theatre credits include *Soldiers* (Finborough Theatre), *Hothouse* (Arcola Theatre & tour), *Troubleshooters* (Soho Theatre), *Julius Caesar* (Barbican), *Electra* (The Gate), *Asylum Monolgues* (Tricycle), *Asylum Dialogues* (New Players), *Danelaw* (White Bear), *Next Door* (Rosemary Branch), *La Bête Humaine* (Grange Court Theatre), *Here But There* (Teatro Vivo), *Two* (Judi Dench Theatre), *Hecuba* (Teatro Technis). TV credits include *EastEnders*, *Casualty*, *Stan*, *True Stories – Elizabeth Fry* (all BBC). Film credits include *Where I Belong*, *All Friends Here*, *The Rat Trap* and *Bloody Mary*. Rebecca works with Actors for Human Rights and is a member of Teatro Vivo.

Rebecca is also a communication skills trainer. In a previous life Rebecca was a light-entertainment agent and has set up and runs Vital Digression, making and producing theatre.

Martin M. Bartelt

Martin started out as a dancer and since has acted, directed and run a theatre. The most recent addition to his professional activities is as a documentary film-maker.

In 2010 Martin edited and was script-consultant for *Con la licencia de Díos*, which won awards at the Doclisboa and Vision du Réel in Nyon. He was assistant to Pina Bausch's Tanztheater Wuppertal, worked with Susanne Linke and was coordinator for the Folkwang University and Dance Archives in Essen, Germany, on several international projects, often in collaboration with the Goethe Institute. An invitation to teach at the Dimitri Theatre School, Verscio, brought him to Switzerland, where he is still based. He is Artistic Director of his theatre company Obviam Est, which he established in 2002, and an international dance and theatre festival in the Italian part of Switzerland. Martin has taught extensively, including stage presence and movement at the University of Hamburg, Germany, masterclasses in physical theatre at the University of Theatre and Cinema in Lisbon, Portugal, and communication skills to business leaders at the University of Social Studies, Olten, Switzerland. He has toured from Ecuador to Belarussia, winning the TeatarFest Award in Sarajevo for the profound humanity of his work *Courage, l'Amour e(s)t la Vie*. He is founder of Artists For The World.

Once the audience is seated, the actor enters.

A year or so after Kate was killed a friend of hers came to stay with me in London and we went out drinking, we went to the Frontline Club, it's a club which was set up in memory of journalists who have died doing their job. The first time I went there I was stunned to see a picture of my sister. There was that picture, the picture I have in my key ring. Months and months after she'd died, there was that picture, in a frame, in a cabinet at the Frontline Club. There she is, just another journalist who has died, important to other journalists, but she's my sister, she's my big sister, who used to have a bath while I sat on the edge and I banged on about…everything. My big sister who wouldn't get up in the morning…although you could possibly tempt her out of bed with a cup of tea. But however much I talk to you about my sister, I can never explain her to you. How do you describe the taste of blueberries to someone who has never eaten blueberries?

Kate was given only four and a half days to prepare to go to one of the – in February 2005 arguably the most dangerous country in the world. Kate said to us that she felt she had to go to prove her commitment to her job. Just before she was asked to go to Somalia she had been told her contract renewal was in question as her commitment was in doubt – she had recently turned down two trips to Iraq... So she agreed to go, though she really didn't want to. Of course, she was an Africa Producer, she chose her life. To quote one of her colleagues, 'You operate on a continent whose recent conflicts include Darfur, Zimbabwe, Congo, Rwanda, Angola. Often you are dependent on local producers to set up things for you, far away and with unreliable telephone communication. Language, logistics and communication are difficult, sometimes impossible, and often do not work out. There are always tight budget restraints. And you are expected to come up with spectacular story ideas that haven't been thought of before. You frequently work with difficult, self-centred correspondents who don't understand the limitations of the environment. And when things go wrong it's the producer who gets the blame. And there is no fame in it – your face rarely appears on TV. This reduces your power in relation to correspondents, simply because they are better known. You are on call twenty-four hours a day, seven days a week. You travel all the time. You burn out easily.' That was Kate's life. The knowledge that she had serious misgivings about the trip on which she died means I sometimes forget that there was so much she loved about her job.

Anyway – we had quite a night at the Frontline Club: lots of journalists, lots of drinking, lots of opinions. All these friends and colleagues of Kate's, so many new stories to hear about her. At the same time, so many questions about that trip to Somalia, everyone aware that this was not her kind of story. She'd interviewed the Rain Queen in South Africa, people living with HIV/AIDS, she had a great focus on women. Then a Somali expert with decades of experience in war zones tells me he would have needed three months to prepare for that trip, rather than the four and a half days Kate was given. And then another foreign correspondent saying he never would have gone, particularly in her circumstances: with only one other colleague – a freelancer – both of them new to the place, and with only a truckload of guys with guns they picked up at the airport for security. And then a BBC correspondent saying that we should let it go, that to continue to ask questions about Kate's deployment was to threaten the future of the BBC's foreign bureaux. Then an ex-BBC journalist asking when we would be suing the BBC, insisting that we should. My head was spinning… Yes, we'd taken on a lawyer, Kate's friends, her colleagues, from various news organisations had repeatedly told us to do so. They told us stories about how unpleasant things had become between news organisations and their dead employees' families…but we weren't wanting to shut down, destroy anything. We wanted our questions answered, we had questions, and it was becoming clear that the only way to get answers out of the BBC was to get our lawyer to ask their lawyers. Not really the way we wanted to do things…

And, it turned out, lots of these guys wanted our questions answered too, but not enough to put their expert opinion on the record. In fact, as my brother and I began researching for the inevitable inquest into Kate's murder we met loads of journalists, many of them really encouraging, saying that something needed to be done about the pressures under which journalists can find themselves. But saying, at the same time, that to talk publicly would be to threaten their careers, their livelihoods. Luckily for us we had nothing to lose.

My brother Charles has described my family as 'industrial consumers of BBC product'. Life-long, ardent fans, of the news mainly, the analysis. The foreign operations of international news organisations are key to keeping global channels of communication open. Democracy is dependent upon this free-flow of information. Journalists will always have to work in unstable places, but how we ask them to do so, this has to be considered. And so the Coroner's decision to look into the planning of Kate's trip, as part of 'how' she died, was vital to help protect journalists who are still alive, working in the field, now. And how marvellous that we had the Coroner we did because it took quite a bit of courage on his part not to cave-in to the enormous pressure from the BBC, whose legal department did not want any of the planning of the trip to be considered as relevant to her murder, let alone whether she felt she had to go to Somalia to keep her job.

The guy with the gun who shot my sister in the back, he killed Kate. Nobody else killed Kate. This ordinary bloke on the streets of Mogadishu, he killed Kate. The BBC did not kill Kate, her colleagues did not kill her, her boss, with whom she had a very difficult relationship at this time, did not kill Kate. And we wanted to sit down, to consider what could be learnt, because that's all you're left with.

But the continual stress of nearly four years' researching for the inquest was extraordinary; I nearly broke under it. I just wanted it to stop, yet I was obsessed with the inquest. It was all I thought about, my friends will tell you it was certainly all I talked about. We knew we'd never get to bring to justice, whatever that means, the guy who killed my sister. Maybe he just needed to pay the rent. Who knows whether he's still alive. It's been reported that the warlord who local specialists believe ordered Kate's killing was bombed and killed himself by the Americans…

I wouldn't want anyone to think that I consider my sister's death there to be any more important than the death of another 39-year-old woman in Somalia. It's more touching to me, but then she's my sister. But the extraordinary press reaction when one, white, blonde Western woman is killed throws into stark relief the deafening silence when day after day after day people die in Somalia at the hands of other people and…for no good reason.

I was working the day Kate was shot – not nice acting work like this, but what I call 'money work'. Basically I turn up at a hotel, smartly dressed – nothing like that, Mum told me not to – and I go, 'coffee, croissants, toilets. Coffee on your right, croissants on your left, toilets straight ahead. Er, no, down there…down there sir…yes, that's it…yes…where it says 'toilets'!' So I spend all day doing that, really, and various other things, sometimes I do some stapling… and I don't know if any of you guys have ever tried this, [I don't know if this has got to *town where show is being performed*] but sometimes I do some photocopying…

Mum had called. She was in Johannesburg where she'd gone to be on holiday with my sister. And then Kate had been sent to Somalia and so Mum was at my sister's house, on holiday, on her own, in Johannesburg. We had a chat. And I'd had to go out for something. It was a beautiful day, the 9th February 2005… pretty chilly, but not a cloud in the sky…and I'd just got back to my desk when someone came through from reception to tell me Mum was on the phone again. What? So I go and pick up the phone and I'm like, 'WHAT?' And my Mum says, 'It's bad news.' And I can hear from her voice…that she's not joking… She says, 'Kate's been shot.' …

I suppose I must have asked whether she was alive or dead, and she was alive. And…I said, I'll get onto it. And then all these phone calls started. I could take you through it call by call…but I'm not going to. The most important call was to our brother to tell him that his sister had been shot…he didn't even know she was in Somalia, so it was a bit of a shock for him… Of course, I phoned my director – I was doing a play at the time, it was a Wednesday and we were finishing on the Saturday. I phoned

Alastair, 'My sister's been shot and I'm not sure what's going to happen but you might need to find someone to replace me. …Alastair?' A bit of a shock for him.

All this information was coming, but all that mattered was that she was okay and she was going to be okay. And, at first light tomorrow, it was already dark in Mogadishu by this point and you can't fly at night there, it's too dangerous, so tomorrow the UN would airlift her out to Johannesburg or to Nairobi.

And you know, during all of this it never even crossed my mind to do a deal with God for Kate's life. If there is a fairy in the sky who does listen to my prayer to save my sister, what about the Libyan mother whose fifteen-year-old boy went out with the rebels six weeks ago and she's not heard from him since?

(Whichever is the latest humanitarian world disaster can be inserted here to make it relevant to that day's audience.)

What about her prayer? That's some kind of, sorry, fucked-up fairy…in my opinion.

Jobi, the manager of the hotel, lovely guy, he comes and asks if I would like some lunch. 'Er…' 'Would you like a sandwich?' 'Er…' 'If you wanted a sandwich, which sandwich would you like?' 'Er… Cheese, please.' And off he goes and brings me a cheese sandwich, which seemed like the right sandwich for the situation…and the cheese sandwich and I just eyeball one another.

Then they let me leave work early! But, of course, the staff, 'That's the least we can do. Her sister's been *shot. Shot?* Yeah, *shot.*' They can see that Kate might die. Of course, I'm focusing very hard on her being alive. Not because I believe I can wish it or will it into being, but because, do you know what? You can't prepare for disaster. Oh, you can maybe get sandbags, that kind of disaster, but emotional disaster, really, there's nothing you can do. I mean, long term you can make sure you have good friends around you, get enough sleep, eat your greens – all the things your mum told you. But short term…? And, it would have seemed very melodramatic to me to focus on the fact that she might die.

My friend Nick is giving me and my brother a lift to the theatre, so we meet at Nick's office. But then Charlie remembers he's got to take some books back to the library on Charing Cross Road – just round the corner. So he goes off to do that. Then Nick's driving me down the Charing Cross Road and I phone my mother in Jo'burg. We're talking – when she *(Nasty sound.)*…and I know that Kate's dead. And what my mother saw in that moment was my uncle coming into the room – just from the look on his face she knew Kate was dead. And I let out this visceral noise, Nick nearly crashes the car: it's very busy – cyclists, buses, tourists – it's rush-hour on the Charing Cross Road. I'm apologising 'I'm sorry, I'm sorry', he's driving and, well, we've had enough death for one day. I was like, 'Pull over, pull over!' 'cause I can see a space. And he pulls over. Actually, it's got loads of red lines – he probably got a ticket…

I get out of the car and I run back up the Charing Cross Road, to the library. And my brother is standing over there by the counter and – I don't want to do him a disservice, but he's probably paying some kind of fine – I stand in the doorway, and I have this moment where I get to decide how to tell my brother his sister is dead,…and I'm not proud of myself, but I just shout 'She's dead!' And the whole place turns to me. And there's this book detector arch thing, so he approaches the book detector arch, and I approach the book detector arch, and we embrace under the book detector in the Charing Cross Road Library.

It was clear to me, now, that I'd finish the show: I didn't have to go to Nairobi, things wouldn't change, Kate couldn't die again. The guys I was doing the play with, to them, it's like me saying,

'Yeah, I'm gonna, I'm gonna go and do my driving test, yeah. I'm just gonna go and do it 'cause I've got it booked.' And everyone's kind of going, 'Maybe you should rebook it?' And they can all see that in you, and it's all over you, it colours you, you're covered in it, like sticky custard, like some sticky custard of death, I'm covered in it, everyone can see it but I, I can't see it. But of course they are all looking at me, looking at me like that. 'Don't think you should do it, Bex,' Alastair says. 'Look, we'll cancel the show for tonight and I have found somebody else for tomorrow so you can go.' … It's such a relief that he's found someone else – and a tiny little bit of me is hurt that I'm so easily replaced.

My life had suddenly veered off, and this day that started, in a very clear vision in my mind of my life on tracks, literally on tracks: I'm on a railway line, that's my life. Suddenly, in the moment of Kate's death, a great big glass wall drops, and there are two sets of tracks and I can see my old life, on the other side of the glass, and I watch it. For a while it runs together; in my diary, I see it. I was meant to be having lunch with my friend Trev the next day, and I never did have lunch with Trev the next day… And they start pulling apart, inexorably, and I don't want it to happen, but there's nothing I can do. And I go off on this life, and I can still see my old life through the glass, but it pulls away, sailing off, into the distance. And I'm on these, frankly inferior tracks, that I didn't want, that are completely unknown and I saw it then, and for a long time afterwards, the cutting and the tracks, and I thought, this is it, I'm not coming back to finish the show.

I've been on the phone to Roger, my sister's fiancé, all day. Turns out he was at the BBC in London, I didn't even know he was in England. … Journalists! So he's coming round to my flat. He is on the phone in the kitchen talking French, talking Lingala – he's Congolese – 'Ma femme est morte, ma femme est morte.' And this is somebody whose father was murdered, was shot in a political assassination, and here he is reliving it. In my kitchen. 'Ma femme est morte, ma femme est morte' to his siblings who've never even met Kate, 'Ma femme est morte, ma femme est morte, ma femme est morte…', over and over and over again…

Up in the sitting room, it's all over the telly, it's heading up the evening news. And there's that picture, – the picture I have in my key ring. Actually it's quite a good picture, which is nice…and surprising, because it's her security pass photo and normally we look like mass-murderers in those. And the phones, they don't stop. At one point I have my friend Kirstie on the landline and our friend Caroline on my mobile, and I do this *(Gesture.)*, put them onto one another and so they can chat in my hand while I discuss something with Charlie.

I don't know, we went to bed about two. And I was woken about 7am, because I always have the radio on, it's the *Today* programme, and it's Fergal Keane talking about my sister. So I email the *Today* programme, 'Dear Sir/Madam, I am Rebecca Peyton, Kate Peyton's sister. Would you be very kind and ask Fergal Keane to give me a ring. Yours faithfully…' And Fergal Keane calls me, and he said he's coming round. And I go

into the bathroom and I look in the mirror…
and it's my sister's face looking back at me.

When I opened the door to Fergal we both
had quite a shock, really. Fergal, because I look
so much like Kate. In fact it's Fergal's reaction
in this moment which means that in future,
whenever I meet a friend of Kate's for the first
time, I warn them in advance that I look a lot
like her, because it's pretty dispiriting when
someone claps eyes on you for the first time,
and they just go 'WAH!' It really isn't good
for my ego. And, of course, Fergal is a famous
journalist: THE Fergal Keane. And here he
is standing on my doorstep. Yes! What a pity
Kate had to die to bring him here… And Fergal
said he couldn't understand why Kate was in
Somalia.

Later that day, I go against everything mother ever told me and accept a lift from a man I hardly know, but Fergal had been so keen to give me a lift to the airport… So we're at Heathrow, having tea and biscuits, and Fergal's phoning in an obituary to a major national newspaper. Kate had obituaries in all the broadsheets. She would have loved it…if she'd been alive…but she's dead. And it's not sinking in at all. For me, I'm sure it must be different for each of us, but for me I think it will take the rest of my life. But now, just twenty-four hours after we got the news, it's too surreal.

The BBC are flying Charlie and me first class to Johannesburg. And the cabin crew are fantastic. I mean, maybe they know our circumstances, or maybe it's just what first class is like, but they cannot do enough for us. And we get giggly because they are so…obsequious, and there's Johnnie Walker Blue label on the menu… None of which stops my big brother getting tearful, saying, 'I just keep thinking I've lost my oldest friend'. And that's true for me too, but what good are we to one another, marooned as we are on our separate islands of grief?

And I want to stay in this aeroplane forever, suspended above my life. I don't ever want to land. I don't know what's going to happen on the other side of all of this. I have a sense, I know the truth, I know she's dead. I kind of knew I'd gradually get skinned, tiny bit by tiny bit my life will be stripped away from me in tiny pieces. Yet I'm hurtling through the air, being pushed against my will into my future, a future which is of no interest to me.

People would go on to comfort us by telling us Kate was still with us, watching over us. Oh, how I envy those people! Because for me, the dead are dead – they seem to have more important things to do than give you a lift, or 'Could you get a pint of milk on the way home? Ah no, sorry, you're dead, aren't you? Not to worry'. My Dad, since he died, he hasn't done a thing for me. He hasn't told me I look pretty, he's not helped me put up any shelves, and he didn't lend me any money for my flat. He's useless. He's just a snatched piece of tune in the back of my memory.

And then, one day, I think it was a Wednesday, the day after the memorial, a week since my sister had died. And there was some, suddenly, I mean, people were coming in and out – constantly – of the house, but people we knew.

Turning up. And then there was this woman we didn't know standing in my sister's sitting room, you kind of walk straight into the sitting room through the doors from the garden. And this woman looked somewhat perplexed, she probably worked out that this chaos wasn't actually a party. And she said, 'Hi.' She said, 'My team have cleaned the swimming pool, er, is Miss Peyton around…for the money?' So we have to explain to her that in fact Miss Peyton is dead. A bit of a shock for her. So she's thinking, 'Oh, hell. What am I going to do about the money? Note to self, next time, before cleaning the pool, check that the person who pays for the pool to be cleaned is still alive before cleaning it.' I would've thought it was page one of the manual, but what would I know? Anyway we scrabble through our handbags and pockets and find some money. And then she says, 'Er, we normally come once a week…just thinking about next week…would it be…convenient?' Oh, that's a difficult question about the future. 'Well, yeah, no, I think so, that would be, yes, I mean, we don't really know where we're going to be you see, obviously we don't want the pool to get dirty – do stop crying! *(To imaginary person in chair crying.)* – it's a very nice pool, so, yeah, and, oh, it's a BBC house, so even if we're no longer here, somebody will be…and anyway Kate would not have wanted the pool to be dirty!' And off she goes. And we just collapsed in giggles because it's such a ridiculous situation. Some small place that my sister occupied – the payment of the swimming pool cleaners – had closed up because she had gone. I would find myself saying, 'I don't think Kate would like… whatever' and then I'd catch myself and go, 'Well, who cares what Kate would like, she's not here, she doesn't have a say any more. The dead do not get a vote in my democracy.' And then, the thing that is gone when somebody dies is the future you…I had with her.

She didn't even send a birthday card. I was angry, I was hurt…it made no difference that she died six weeks before my birthday… It has to be said though that my friends made a huge fuss of me, probably more than if my sister had *not* been murdered. My party was at a nightclub in Brixton in south London and I managed to get thrown out. I got into a bit of a barney with the doorman, I was just telling him what I thought of him – I was very concise – and he won't let me back in, despite my running and hurling myself at the door, which I was sure would work. It doesn't, in fact. He's throwing me out. Oo, you should know what I was wearing. I was wearing a black chain-mail top, well a front really, the back was just string, and a mini-skirt, micro mini. Not suitable for winter in England, not suitable for a 33-year-old – a look I think my mother would describe as cheap. I try to explain myself to his colleague through my tears, *(Drunken stumbling around, including tears.)* 'I'm sorry about all that. All got a bit arrrrrgh. Can I go back in? No. My keys are in there. My money is in there, my phone is in there, my friends are all in there… Can I go back in? Are you chilly? It's a bit chilly. No. Well, that's a nice coat. Do you use it for, is it a work coat, do you, you could wear it for, you know, meals out? U-huh. My coat is in there. Can I go back in? I need a bit of a wee. Can I go in for a bit of a wee?… My sister was murdered six weeks ago…can I go back in?' No, it turns out I could not go back in. So I go and sit in what, I believe, is the traditional place for the miserably drunk and tearful, known by the French as le gutter. I have, by the way, since perfected the art of getting what I want *because* my sister was murdered, and I can tell you it works particularly well with plumbers in east London.

And that really marked the beginning of a solid eighteen month period of drinking and partying in a desperate attempt to escape to oblivion rather than stay in reality, rather than be in my own skin. And during the time I was drinking too much I was just longing for Kate to turn up and disapprove. Although, because our father died when we were small we've always had an… alternative attitude to death in our family, so Kate probably wouldn't have disapproved at all.

I mean, I can't imagine why I can't talk about death…for example, at dinner parties. People believe you can provoke somebody's death just by mentioning it. But I believe you can disempower something by naming it. Talk about your fear and it might just dissipate. So, I want to talk about things that matter and I want to listen, and engage with discussions about death, destruction and…liver disease! But mostly I am just…staggeringly inappropriate.

A week after Kate died her suitcase came back to Jo'burg – it was a big, green Samsonite thing, and she kind of lived out of it. For a woman who refused to carry a handbag she had a damn big suitcase. When my aunt and I opened it… Kate was asthmatic, so her puffers and all her underwear…and whatever book she was reading that she wouldn't finish any more…her recording equipment, her camera. In the middle of the case, was a wrapped parcel. And I realised that it must be the clothes she'd been shot in. I didn't open them then. I mean, I didn't want to unpack her case at all because I would have not done it when she was alive. So if I unpack her stuff, then she's dead…

A couple of days later, on the phone to Em, I decided, out of nowhere, to unpack it. It was this white sheet on the outside, then a white plastic packet, and then the clothes, all neatly folded, and with such care… Her shirt, with a tiny little bullet-hole in the back, blood around it…dried blood, now. Her trousers…with blood on them…and her walking boots…with blood on them. And I've still got the clothes in my flat and I'll keep them…for as long as I keep them. I will not turn away from how my sister died.

Back in the UK there was so much to organise for the funeral – musicians, caterers, portaloos – and then I get a call from Roger. Nine of his siblings are trying to get the papers to come from Kinshasa and they just can't get them. Of course, it isn't the government of the Democratic Republic of the Congo that are stopping them coming, it's my government, the British government, that are stopping them coming. Roger's life has just been destroyed by these events and his brothers and sisters want to come to give him a hug, and…I'm staggered at the sheer racism I know is unfolding. The entirety of my South African family have just walked straight in for the funeral, they're more than welcome, but these other Africans, no, no, they can't come in. My family, fifteen white South Africans, oh no, fifteen white South Africans and one black one – just for luck – can come right in, no problem, more than welcome. Roger's brothers and sisters, on the other hand, all of whom have husbands, children, businesses to run back in the Congo, no, they can't come. And what's the difference? These other Africans, well, they're just a little bit too…black. And there's nothing I can do. There is nothing I can do to persuade my government of the goodwill of Roger's family: that they will come for the funeral, give him a hug and go home. They're not going to disperse to Colchester to clean toilets for two pounds an hour until they get their papers in ten years' time.

In the end two of Roger's relations are allowed to come from Kinshasa and some of his European family come to support him. And the people in my village were great, they had our friends and family to stay over the funeral. Graham and Barbara were particularly good and warmly welcomed Roger's family into their home… grown-ups and kids. And I say they were particularly good because the Congolese did not speak English and Graham and Barbara did not speak French or Lingala – they are English after all, we don't need other languages. And a while after the funeral, Graham told me this story, that the day after the funeral, the Sunday, Graham had been alone in the hall when one of their enormous dogs had come tripping through the house with a pair of knickers hanging out of his mouth. Red skimpy knickers. Not Barbara's knickers. So Graham wrestled the knickers away from the dog, and then, he thought, 'Oh my God! I was standing there and had these knickers in my hand and any minute they might come home and they'd think I'd been going through their underwear.' So he went upstairs to put them back. But when he got upstairs he didn't know which room they'd come out of. By this stage these infernal knickers were burning a hole in his hand. So…he just threw them into a room and slammed the door and nothing was said about it…probably because nobody could say anything about it because nobody had a language in common.

People turned up at my Mum's back door, 'It's shepherd's pie. You just need to put it in the oven', 'Oh, thank you. Another shepherd's pie'. People are amazing.

On the Saturday morning, the morning of the funeral, I'm up and there's this whole problem with getting the Congolese Salvation Army Band from London up to Suffolk for the funeral, some problem with the van hire.

'Yes, I know, but I've got a credit card. I do, but I'm in Suffolk now. I know… I can bring cash next week, say Tuesday, Wednesday? … I can't sign, I'm not in London now… Please, it's for my sister's funeral…she was *murdered*!' It didn't work. We have to resign ourselves: no Congolese music.

I very much wanted to see Kate's body, Mum didn't and Charles did. So we entered into really protracted negotiations with the undertakers, they asked us if we realized that – she'd been overnight in Mogadishu…unrefrigerated. In the end we go to see Kate. There's the coffin, obviously an open coffin, and she's in this white satiny, sheety thing, and I see her face, her hands, her hair…and she looked just like Kate, only dead. In my experience that's what dead people tend to look like… And they have done an amazing job with the make-up. She wasn't really into make-up when she was alive. Looking good now! I got to see my sister, I got to touch her hands and her face, and her hair, and she is cold, not room temperature – she's refrigerated now. And I'm glad I saw her because I know she's not somewhere suffering, she is definitely dead.

Still by the morning of the funeral, I had not resolved the on-going wrangle with my mother about what I was going to wear for the funeral. Kate had this gorgeous green designer evening dress, off-the-shoulder-to-the-floor, I looked fantastic in it… I really wanted to wear this dress. I hadn't known about it when she was alive – and I wanted to ask her about it – but all I had left was the dress. Mum really was not into the idea of my wearing what was essentially an evening dress to a daytime funeral. So I'd put it on, I think, the day before and showed Rachel and Emma. And they were going, 'Wow, you look gorgeous! … We can see why your mum doesn't want you to wear it.' I was like, 'No, no, no! I want to wear it!' And I didn't even know why I wanted to wear it. I wanted to be stunning. I didn't want to be the least bit funereal. I wanted to be a jarring juxtaposition of foxy and colourful and alive and everybody would go, 'Look what she's wearing…do you think she knows her sister's dead?' It was just a really unreasonable, emotional urge at a time of many, many really unreasonable, emotional urges that rendered me completely inappropriate. So in the end, for world peace in general and peace in a small village in Suffolk in particular, I conceded and wore something else.

And then about 500 people turned up to the funeral. Two coach loads of BBC people came from London – Kate would have been surprised…and touched, I think, although maybe some were the same BBC people who would go on – during the inquest – to threaten us as a family with legal action should we defame anyone related to the BBC… I don't think Kate would have liked that.

And then the Congolese Salvation Army Band turns up! It's the 5th March, the snow's up to here, *(Three inches or so.)* and they've managed to get to Beyton from London in various cars they've borrowed. I cannot imagine how they've managed to do it…and then I see their cars, and…I really can't imagine how they've managed to do it. But they're here in one piece. And their music, Mum had been worried that their music would be too 'churchy' – her word, and she's the Christian in the family – but it's up and vibrant and brings us all together in a dancing mass, people from Suffolk and the Congo, and speaks to me of Africa in my middle-class-white-girl-from-Beyton kind of a way.

At the back of the cathedral we had the Somali flag. It's blue with a white cross… When Kate was killed local Somali people, over night, had sewn this enormous Somali flag. People in Mogadishu have nothing. I mean, they have no peace and they have no security, but also materially… Yet, these people were so disgusted by Kate's murder that they had sewed, over night, a Somali flag to go on her coffin as she was airlifted out of the country…

People are amazing.

Paulina! How could I forget Paulina? Paulina was Kate's housekeeper and great friend of ten years' standing. When we were sorting Kate's stuff in Johannesburg she took nearly all of Kate's shoes. I said, 'Why?' 'cause Kate had size five feet and Paulina's got size three feet. And Paulina said, 'I'm going to wear lots of socks.' So then Paulina took everything we didn't bring back to England, either Paulina could use it or someone in her township could use it. And I like the thought that somewhere in South Africa someone's chopping carrots on Kate's chopping board...now.

The applause is interrupted as the actor fetches a list which has been on the table beside her, appearing maybe to be a mat for the jug and glass. She reads:

'This show is dedicated to the following journalists who died in *[Year]* on account of their jobs:

Five journalists are listed in the following format:

NAME, ROLE & COMPANY (IF THERE IS A COMPANY), COUNTRY.

…and to their families.'

I don't know about you, but I need a drink.

See you in the bar.

The actor exits.

The End.